CW00735105

North-West England

Simon Kirwan

Text: Liam Kirwan

MYRIAD
LONDON

Cheshire, the Wirral & Manchester

Characterised by its geological features of red sandstone and long, golden sandy beaches, the Wirral peninsula is an environment of natural beauty, wildlife and small picturesque villages. Surrounded by the river Dee to the south, the river Mersey to the north, and the Irish Sea to the west, the area has its own distinct identity and a rich cultural history. Along with the neighbouring county of Cheshire, the region is a rural haven with areas of international ecological importance. From the dense woodland of Delamere to the craggy, coastal hillside of Thurstaston, it can almost be seen as England in miniature. The great city of Manchester with its historic centre and array of cultural attractions is within close reach.

The Dee estuary

Hilbre is the largest of a group of three tidal islands that lie at the mouth of the Dee estuary. The others are Little and Middle Eye – Little Eye, the smallest of the three, is the first reached when walking from the mainland at West Kirby. The islands are cut off from the mainland by the tide for up to five hours out of every 12; it is thought that these rocky outcrops were part of the mainland until the end of the last ice age, when melting ice led to increased water levels. The glorious red rock from which the islands are formed is Bunter Sandstone, which can also be found on the mainland and forms a rocky ridge down to Thurstaston. With the land around the islands alternating between submersion by sea water and exposure, the rocky shores have a unique mix of plants and animal species. Hilbre Island observatory was established in 1957 to monitor bird migration patterns.

Thurstaston
below

A village on the Wirral peninsula between Heswall and Caldy, Thurstaston has a magnificent beach stretching along the banks of the Dee estuary. Many of the pebbles and small boulders that litter the beach were brought to the area by melting glaciers during the last ice age and can be traced from as far away as the Lake District and Scotland. The wide variety of terrain at Thurstaston provides a range of habitats for flora and fauna alike. Close to the beach, wildflowers such as oxeye daisies thrive on the grassy hillocks, which throughout the summer months are ablaze with colour. Looking out across the Dee estuary, the Clwydian Hills of north Wales can be seen clearly in the distance.

Parkgate *left*

At one time Parkgate, just north of Neston, was a popular seaside resort and one of the main departure points for ships sailing to Ireland. However, the progressive silting of the Dee estuary saw the town's sands become consumed by grass and, with no access to the beach, the once fashionable resort fell into decline. During the Second World War, decoy lights were placed across the marshes here to confuse German bombers into thinking they were heavily-populated settlements. Nowadays, the marshes are part of an RSPB nature reserve.

Thurstaston Hill *below left*

This modest hill is just 255ft (90m) above sea-level but from its summit visitors can enjoy one of the best views across the Wirral and the Dee estuary. On a clear day you can see both Liverpool cathedrals, Blackpool Tower, Formby Point, the Clwydian Hills and the north Wales coast, and even the Snowdonia National Park. Thurstaston is home to a large red stone outcrop known locally as Thor's Stone. Some say the stone was raised by the Danes to commemorate a great battle, while others suggest it was the site of ritual sacrifices made to Thor by the Vikings. The Vikings certainly settled across this area and may well have celebrated their rituals here, but the more likely explanation is that this unusual outcrop is simply a glacial erratic.

Beeston Castle *above*

Perched majestically atop Beeston Crag, the striking ruins of Beeston Castle stand at over 500ft (152m) on an outcrop of red sandstone. The origins of the building date back to 1226, when Ranulf, Earl of Chester, decided to build an impregnable fortress to defend the Welsh border. The castle design is, unusually for an English castle, of Saracen influence, possibly due to the fact that Ranulf spent time in Syria during the Crusades. Aside from the natural defences provided by the steep hill, it was extremely well fortified. It fell into disrepair during the 16th century but, with the outbreak of the Civil War, it was quickly brought back into use as a Royalist stronghold.

Frodsham *left*

Looking down onto the small market town of Frodsham, the horizon is dominated by the cooling towers of Fiddlers Ferry power station. One of its eight towers collapsed in January 1984, due to the freak high winds of that winter, but it has since been rebuilt. The raking M56 motorway viaduct dissects the landscape, separating the redbrick residential area from the oil and chemical industries to the west. The river Weaver flows through the outskirts of the town and into the estuary of the river Mersey. In the 19th century much of the land surrounding the town was marsh and it is this drained area that has provided land for agricultural and industrial use. The town nestles in the shelter of Overton Hill, which at one time was a popular destination for visitors from Liverpool and the surrounding area. The "Overton pleasure grounds" had tea shops, fairground attractions and donkey rides and were famous throughout the north-west.

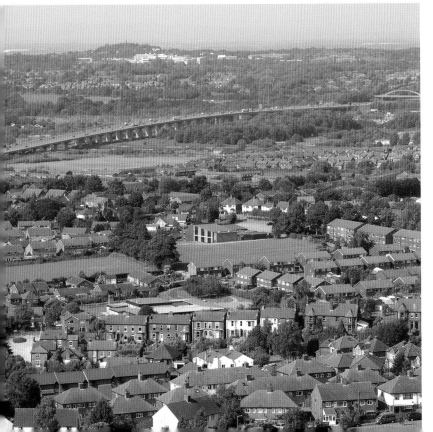

Salford Quays *below*

The bold glass and metallic structures that rise from the old docklands symbolise the regeneration that has taken place in Salford Quays. With an eclectic mix of bars, cafes, restaurants and cultural attractions, the once derelict waterfront has been transformed, turning a wasteland into a major tourist attraction. Its success has led to the fastest drop in unemployment in the Greater Manchester region; amazingly, more people now work on the site than in its heyday as a seaport. The Victoria Harbour Building illustrates how the modern Quays complement the historic waterfront of the old docklands. Located at the heart of the redevelopment of Salford Quays, the Lowry Centre has given a home to creativity, entertainment and the performing arts.

Manchester Central Library *right*

In the first rank of the city's most recognisable and famous landmarks, Manchester's Central Library which dominates St Peter's Square is one of the largest lending and reference libraries outside London. Designed in a classical style by the architect E Vincent Harris, the foundation stone was laid in 1930 by the Prime Minister Ramsay MacDonald and building work was completed four years later. This wonderful aerial view of the building allows a rare glimpse of the large domed glass roof which covers the central reading room, a feature obscured from street level by the higher surrounding lead-covered roof. The library holds a large collection of books in Chinese languages, reflecting the significant Chinese population of Chinatown and Greater Manchester.

The Lowry
Footbridge *below*

The centrepiece of Salford Quays is the spectacular lifting footbridge which spans the Manchester Ship Canal and links the Lowry Centre with Trafford Wharfside and the site of the Imperial War Museum North. Completed in June 1999, the 300ft (92m) long bridge provides pedestrian and cycle access across the canal while continuing to allow the flow of shipping, thanks to a vertical lifting design which raises the bridge 75ft (23m). The Lowry Centre gave a permanent home to the works of LS Lowry, and also provides a performance space for drama, dance and music. Designed by renowned architect Daniel Libeskind, the Imperial War Museum North opened in July 2002.

West Lancashire, Fylde & Merseyside

There can be few places with such a wide range of scenery and terrain as this region of Lancashire. From the hustle and bustle of Liverpool and the seaside towns of Blackpool and Southport to the tranquillity of small villages and inland waterways it is an area of constant change and surprise. As the flat coastal land rises up into the west Lancashire hills, the region can perhaps best be appreciated from the top of Parbold Hill. Looking west the view takes in the coast out towards Southport and the Irish Sea or turn to the north and look out over High Moor (bottom) and the rolling west Lancashire plains. Near the summit of Parbold Hill stands the Parbold Bottle (below), a stone monument which was built to celebrate the passing of the Reform Act in 1832. It was rebuilt in 1958.

Glasson Dock *above*

Today it is a busy port and yachting marina, but just over 200 years ago the area where the village of Glasson Dock now stands would have been little more than rough pasture and wetlands. When the larger shipping vessels found that navigation through the shallow waters of the Lune Channel into the Lancaster Quays was becoming increasingly difficult, Parliament instructed the Port Commission to remedy the problem. By 1779 the Commission decided to build a wet dock at Glasson and by 1787 the first ship, the *Mary*, docked at the newly created Glasson Dock. By 1834, with a small village community now established around the dock, Glasson's first shipyard opened, along with other port buildings including a Customs House and Watch House. A branch railway to Lancaster followed shortly afterwards; now closed, today it is a well-liked walking and cycle route. While Glasson Dock is a popular visitor attraction, it remains a thriving working dock. It handles over 150,000 tonnes of cargo annually, shipping out coal to the Isle of Man and the Outer Hebrides while handling the inward traffic of fertiliser and animal foodstuffs.

Skippool *above*

Once a lively port, ships from Russia and Barbados would unload their exotic cargoes of wine, sugar, rum and tobacco at Skippool. By the middle of the 19th century the volume of traffic at Skippool and nearby Wardleys exceeded that of Liverpool but gradually Fleetwood, with its ability to handle larger ships and its links to the railway, rendered Skippool obsolete. Today, ramshackle jetties and assorted nautical craft in varying states of repair are tethered to the moorings at Skippool Creek.

Pilling *right*

The village of Pilling is located on the northern coast of the Fylde peninsula between Fleetwood and Lancaster. It is separated from the Irish Sea by an extensive area of marsh and mossland which provides a unique habitat for plants and wildlife and is regarded as one of the region's finest bird-watching sites.

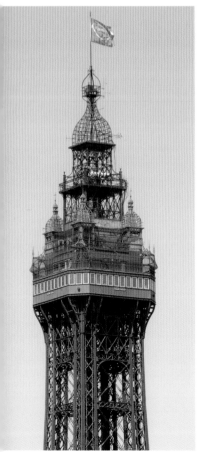

Blackpool *above & left*

The Golden Mile at Blackpool is the stretch of promenade between the town's North and Central Piers and it has been a magnet for holidaymakers and day-trippers since the late 19th century. The advent of the railways enabled the factory workers of Lancashire to descend on the town during the traditional "wakes weeks" and swap the grime of industrial cotton towns for clean air and seaside fun. With its Winter Gardens, Pleasure Beach and Tower, Blackpool could cater for up to 250,000 visitors at a time. The Tower itself, at 519ft (158m) tall, was inspired by the Eiffel Tower in Paris and cost £42,000 to construct; it first opened to the public on 14 May 1894. A Grade 1 listed building, it is normally painted dark red but for its centenary celebrations in 1994 it was painted gold.

Lytham St Anne's *below*

Built in 1805 on what is now Lytham Green, the windmill, which is close to the promenade, is Lytham St Anne's most famous landmark. One of several mills on the Fylde, it was fully operational until 1919 when a fire destroyed most of the internal workings. Rebuilt and renovated, the mill now houses a museum chronicling its history. Next door is the old Lytham Lifeboat House, which is now the Lifeboat Museum. The Shipwrecked Mariners Society were responsible for the first lifeboat stationed at Lytham in 1851 and, in the years since, the lifeboats at Lytham have been responsible for saving hundreds of lives.

Ashurst Beacon *above*

Ashurst Beacon was erected in 1798 by Sir William Ashurst as part of a Lancashire chain of signalling bonfires to form a communication link from Everton Beacon in Liverpool to Lancaster Castle. It was built specifically to warn of invasion by the French during the Napoleonic "scare", when Bonaparte was massing his troops at Boulogne. The beacon is the highest point of the Upholland ridge, and on a clear day it is possible to see the national parks of Snowdonia, the Lake District, the Peak District and the Yorkshire Dales. The chain of beacons could be seen by ships on the Irish Sea and was a useful visual aid for seamen.

Rufford *above*

At the West Lancashire village of Rufford, the Rufford branch of the Leeds & Liverpool Canal breaks away to join up with the river Douglas; it is regarded as one of the most beautiful sections of the region's waterways. Also known as the Lower Douglas Navigation, this 11-mile stretch of canal runs from Burscough Bridge to the river Ribble estuary. The popularity of this stretch of waterway is emphasised by the newly-built marina at Fettlers Wharf which can accommodate nearly 100 boats. The lock at Rufford is one of seven well-preserved locks on this stretch that enable boats to navigate the changing terrain.

Jenny Brown's Point *left*

Just south of the village of Silverdale lies Jenny Brown's Point, and from here there are splendid panoramic views south across the bay from Clougha all the way round to Black Combe in Cumbria. Morecambe, Lancaster and Heysham are all visible on clear days. The origins of the unusual place name are said to relate to the story of a local woman, a nanny called Jenny Brown, who drowned while trying to save her children.

Marshside *above*

The mudflats and sands of Marshside are situated at the southern outer shore of the Ribble estuary. More than 40,000 birds over-winter here and there is an RSPB reserve. This was originally a district where fishermen lived; many of their cottages can still be seen today.

Ribble *right*

The Ribble rises in the heart of North Yorkshire and flows through Lancashire. It finally reaches the coast and creates the estuary between Southport and Blackpool. Regarded by many as the most important river estuary in the United Kingdom, it is the winter home to over a quarter of a million birds each year.

Formby Point *left & right*

A distinctive feature of the north-west coast, Formby Point is the tip of land jutting out to sea, marking the area where the Irish Sea meets the Mersey Estuary. Formby has England's largest undeveloped sand dune system and is a vital habitat for a wide range of wildlife. The most common dune plant is marram grass, which serves a crucial role in holding the sand together and helps in the constant battle against coastal erosion. However, it is this very erosion that has recently revealed the footprints of people, cattle, deer, dogs and birds, thought to date back between 3,500 and 6,500 years.

Southport Pier and beach *above & below*

Built in 1860, Southport Pier has seen more than its share of incidents ranging from storm damage to fires to the threat of demolition. It was originally 3600ft (1097m) long but was extended in 1868 to 4380ft (1335m), but a fire in 1959 reduced it to its present length of 3650ft (1112m). However, it is still the second longest pier in the country, and the oldest iron pleasure pier in existence. By 1990, with the pier having fallen into disrepair, Sefton Council applied to have the Grade II listed structure demolished. It was saved due to the action of local pressure groups with a motion to demolish it being defeated by a single vote. Subsequently, funding was obtained to provide a £7m refurbishment, returning the pier to its former glory. Today, the skeletal form of the Traumatizer rollercoaster at Southport's Pleasureland fairground still dominates the skyline. Sadly, Pleasureland is no more, victim to changing tastes and competition from rival attractions. Its closure marked the end of nearly 100 years of fairgrounds in Southport.

Liverpool, William Brown Street *right*

The City of Liverpool famously lays claim to more listed buildings than any other British city outside London and has more Georgian buildings than Bath. This fine architectural heritage is highlighted in the cultural quarter around William Brown Street, where the neo-classical buildings of Liverpool's World Museum and the adjacent Central Library building sit opposite the magnificent St George's Hall and the Alfred Waterhouse-designed North Western Hotel. The hotel was opened in 1867 to serve the passengers using Liverpool's Lime Street station and its grand and imperious design complemented the adjacent terminus. It fell into disrepair but has now been restored and is once again a vibrant building, in its new role as halls of residence to students of Liverpool John Moores University. Similarly, the World Museum, with its imposing Corinthian columns, reflects the 19th-century prosperity of Liverpool; it has recently re-opened to the public following a £35m refurbishment. The museum's extensive collections cover archaeology, ethnology and the natural and physical sciences, a Natural History Centre and a free Planetarium. In 2004, the City of Liverpool was granted World Heritage status. The area covered includes the cultural quarter around William Brown Street, the Pier Head, the Albert and Stanley Docks, the commercial centre and the warehouses and merchants' houses of Duke Street.

Liverpool Metropolitan Cathedral *above*

The unusual design of the Roman Catholic or Metropolitan Cathedral, coupled with Liverpool's strong Irish connections, has led the building to be affectionately known by locals as "Paddy's Wigwam". Originally the building was to be a grand classical structure designed by Sir Edwin Lutyens, to mirror the neo-gothic Anglican cathedral at the opposite end of the aptly named Hope Street. However, financial restrictions led to the abandonment of this grandiose structure after completion of the crypt in 1941. Instead, the construction of this radical design by Sir Frederick Gibberd was undertaken, its circular shape allowing congregation and clergy to be more closely integrated. Just five years after building work started the cathedral was completed and consecrated in May 1967.

Liverpool Waterfront

When Prince Albert opened the Albert Dock in 1846 he was moved to say: "I have heard of the greatness of Liverpool but the reality far surpasses the expectation." How many thousands of sailors and passengers, when arriving in Liverpool for the first time, must have echoed those sentiments as they cast their gaze across the majestic facade of the city's waterfront? Its renowned skyline is defined by the presence of "The Three Graces", the group of buildings which dominate Liverpool's famous Pier Head. To give them their correct names, they are the Royal Liver Building (1908-1911), the Cunard Building (1915) and the Port of Liverpool Building (1907).

The Royal Liver Building *above*

Crowned with the city's famous Liver birds, which spread their wings from high above the two towers, the Royal Liver Building symbolises Liverpool more than any other structure. Its clock faces are actually bigger than those of Big Ben, and were designed so that ships could tell the time as they passed. Made of reinforced concrete – one of the first large-scale buildings to utilise this material – the Royal Liver Building was constructed as the head-quarters of the Royal Liver Friendly Society, a role it fulfils to this day.

East Lancashire

Renowned by locals as Lancashire's hill country, east Lancashire is a region of relatively unsung beauty. From its series of reservoirs close to the West Pennine Moors to its thriving market towns further north, it is laced with heritage and history. Blessed with a unique landscape offering a multitude of habitats to a diverse range of wildlife, this is an area of both national and international environmental importance. Seemingly dominated from all points by the imposing shadow of Pendle Hill, the area's stunning scenery sees leafy lanes meander through a combination of rural woodland and historic villages. At the northern edge of Pendle Hill lies the beautiful village of Downham (below), a rural idyll which remains unspoilt by the passing of time. Regarded by many as the most picturesque of all the Lancashire villages, it has been a popular location for film and television productions, most famously for the 1961 classic *Whistle Down The Wind*.

Pendle Hill

The whale-backed form of Pendle was known to the Celts as simply "the Hill". Seven miles long and varying from one to three miles in width, Pendle rises to 1827ft (557m). From the summit, walkers are rewarded with a magnificent panorama, with views of the Lakeland fells some 60 miles away. Well-worn and established paths to the top of the hill make it a popular choice for fell-walkers and tourists alike, its dramatic appearance and mysterious history drawing visitors from far and wide.

The history of Pendle Hill

Of all the tales of alleged witchcraft in England, the case in the early 17th century of the so-called Pendle Witches is perhaps one of the most infamous events in Lancashire's history. In 1612, 10 men and women were tried and found guilty on trumped-up charges of witchcraft and murder in the Pendle Forest area and hanged at Lancaster Castle. Pendle Hill and the area around it remain closely associated with witches and each Hallowe'en large numbers of visitors make the steep climb to the summit. Forty years later, George Fox ascended the hill and claimed to have witnessed a great vision which led him to found the Quaker movement. According to Fox, he saw "the countryside alive with men, all moving to one place".

Wards Reservoir *above*

The mainly rural village of Belmont still has a reminder of the area's industrial past in the form of the local bleach works; the owners, the Belmont Bleaching and Dyeing Company, also own Wards Reservoir. Known locally as the Blue Lagoon, the reservoir lies on the north-east side of Winter Hill. North of the reservoir near the church is the Potato Pie Path. In the past villagers used this route to transport peat from the moors until landowners attempted to stop the practice by blocking the path. The outraged villagers held a sit-in for a week on the path itself. They were sustained by potato pies from supporters during the sit-in until the landowners relented.

Haslingden Grane *above*

Located in the Rossendale district on the edge of the West Pennine Moors, Haslingden Grane contains three reservoirs built in the 1850s to supply drinking water to the growing industrial towns. The construction of Calf Hey, Ogden and Holden Wood reservoirs led to the displacement of the local villagers. Prior to the flooding of the valley, a community of 1,300 people lived in Haslingden Grane, which although mainly agricultural was also the centre of an illegal whisky distilling industry. Ruined cottages, abandoned farmsteads and old tracks all serve as a reminder of the people who once lived here.

Turton *below*

Originally built during Tudor times, Turton Tower is a Grade I listed building situated close to the edge of the West Pennine Moors. At one time it was home to Sir Humphrey Chetham, the Lancashire treasurer for the Roundhead forces during the Civil War, and the tower itself was used for quartering troops. Set in beautiful woodlands, the distinctive 15th-century country house fell into decline during the Georgian era, but was lovingly restored and extended by the Kay family during the Victorian period. The nine acres of delightful gardens are home to an array of follies and a traditional English country garden. Today, the house features an outstanding collection of furniture, paintings and other artefacts dating from the Renaissance to the present day.

Rivington Pike *above & below*

A prominent point on the Rivington Moors at 1200ft (361m), Rivington Pike has long been used as a beacon point and was first recorded in use as far back as 1588. However, the tower that now stands on the top of the pike was built in 1733 as a shelter for grouse-shooting parties. Although no longer in use, and all entrances having been bricked up, it remains a Grade II listed building. The area was chosen as the location of mountain-bike events during the 2002 Commonwealth Games and is still popular with cyclists.

Jumbles *left*

When the nearby Wayoh reservoir was switched to domestic supply duties, construction work began on the 56-acre Jumbles Reservoir to protect the flow of water through Bradshaw Brook. On its completion in 1971, the Jumbles Country Park was opened. Lying within the Bradshaw valley to the north of Bolton, the park is home to an abundance of plants and wildlife, with wild orchids thriving along the grassy banks. Jumbles itself takes its unusual name from a variation of "dumbles", a northern word for a valley with wooded sides down which tumbles a stream.

Forest of Bowland

Often referred to as Lancashire's "hidden gem", the Forest of Bowland borders the Fylde coast to the west and the Yorkshire Dales to the east. An area of outstanding natural beauty, Bowland is characterised by its striking landscape of remote gritstone fells dissected by slender wooded valleys or cloughs which drain the vast tracts of heather-clad peat moorland. Steeply inclined walls of rock link the desolate high ground moors with the surrounding broad river valleys of the Ribble, Hodder, Wyre and Lune. The picturesque stone hamlets and villages are rich in history, and clues to Bowland's past can be seen throughout the area, from the Roman settlement at Ribchester, to the Saxon place names of Grindleton and Caton and the Norse influences apparent in suffixes such as "beck", "gill" and "dale". Nowhere is history more evident than on the banks of the Ribble, where the weathered and crumbling stones are all that remain of the once magnificent Cistercian Abbey at Sawley (below), shadowed in the distance by the silhouette of Pendle Hill.

Birk Bank *right*

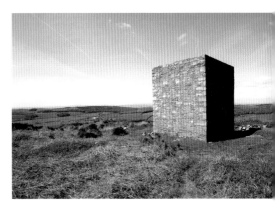

The Forest of Bowland boasts some of the finest grouse moors in Britain, and although the landscape may appear untouched, it is only through careful management of the fells that the population of grouse can be sustained. Situated on the edge of the Clougha access area, Birk Bank is typical of the Bowland fells with its distinctive carpet of heather. This provides feeding and nesting cover for the grouse, while benefiting other birds like the golden plover, curlew and hen harrier. The stone tower pictured provides a fine vantage point during the grouse season and is an ideal starting point for climbing Clougha Pike.

Forest of Bowland *left*

Covering 312 square miles of rural Lancashire and north Yorkshire, much of Bowland is an area of open moorland. The "forest" of its name is derived from the ancient meaning of a "royal hunting ground" and today the majority of the land still belongs to the Crown. In medieval times wild boar, deer, wolves, wild cats and game roamed the forest, but nowadays it is the tranquillity and isolation of this untamed wilderness that define this most beautiful corner of north-west England. Scattered around the edge of the area are a collection of picturesque villages including Slaidburn, Chipping and Downham.

Clougha Pike *below*

Located in the north-western hills of the Forest of Bowland, five miles east of Lancaster, Clougha Pike's distinctive profile looms large over the surrounding area and presents a commanding view over the Lune estuary which lies south of the county town. It is visible from as far away as Barrow-in-Furness and the Old Man of Coniston and gains its name from the series of deeply incised cloughs visible across its flanks. Clougha is part of of an "access area" which, including the Wardstone and Tarnbook areas, covers some 1717 acres of opened-up land. Access areas like this have provided large tracts of open countryside where walkers now have the freedom to roam the moors and fells. Although covered in part by large sections of blanket bog land, the fell is popular as a training ground with fell-runners, and each year the Darren Jones Clougha Pike race takes place across the hill. This challenging fell race covers five miles and includes 1400ft of tough slopes for the runners to ascend and descend.

Ribchester *right*

Over the centuries, the changing course of the river Ribble has all but covered the Roman fort at Ribchester. Located at a junction where the river converged with five major roads, *Bremetenacum Veteranorum,* as it was known to the Romans, consisted of both a fort and civilian village. It was strategically vital to the Romans in Britain, linking Manchester, Chester, Lancaster, York and Hadrian's Wall by road while providing access to the coast via the Ribble. The most significant remains are that of the bath house, discovered in 1837 and located just outside of what would have been the fort walls. There was also a temple, the stone pillars of which are said to form part of the entrance to Ribchester's White Bull Hotel. As the Latin name suggests, the fort would have been a home for veteran soldiers, retired from service who were allowed to farm in the area.

Cromwell Bridge *below left*

Also known as Devil's Bridge, this ruined packhorse bridge on the Lower Hodder dates back to 1562 and was built by Sir Richard Shireburn to replace a 14th-century wooden bridge. It derives its name from the reported crossing by Oliver Cromwell during his march from Skipton to win the decisive Battle of Preston in 1648. It is said that Cromwell led his 4,000 men across the bridge in single file and it took almost a full day for the horses, mules and men to cross the bridge. Close by is the Lower Hodder bridge of 1819.

Stonyhurst College *below*

In the shadow of Longridge Fell, the magnificent Jesuit College at Stonyhurst (established in 1794) is one of the most famous boarding and day schools in the country. As a Catholic institution in the 19th century part of the school's role was to educate older boys ("gentlemen philosophers" as they were called) who were prohibited by law from attending university. Stonyhurst counts Sherlock Holmes' creator Arthur Conan Doyle and the actor Charles Laughton amongst its former pupils. In 1648, when Oliver Cromwell stayed overnight at Stonyhurst prior to marching on Preston, legend has it that the Lord Protector and his troops slept on tables in their full body armour. With building work unfinished at the time, Cromwell pronounced it the finest "half house" he had ever seen.

Trough of Bowland *above*

Lancashire's most renowned pass, the Trough of Bowland is a dramatic and narrow steep-sided valley that was formed at the end of the last ice age. Although appearing untouched by human hand save for the working farmland across its pastures, closer inspection reveals clues to the area's industrial heritage. Quarries, a smelting mill and a limekiln point to a time when Bowland was as much a part of the industrial revolution as the rest of Lancashire.

Wolf Fell *right*

Wolves survived until the 17th century within the Forest of Bowland and their presence is reflected by place names such as "Wolf Hole Crag" and "Wolf Fell". The higher ground was their favoured territory, while deer and game inhabited the lower slopes. Nowadays the area is alive with walkers, taking advantage of the stunning views over neighbouring Parlick Fell and the picturesque village of Chipping, a former wool town.

Cumbria

Home to the Lake District national park and within it England's highest mountain, Scafell Pike, Cumbria contains the most breathtaking and stunning scenery in England. A source of inspiration to poets, writers and artists alike, it is an area of wildly dramatic contrasts from tiny hamlets and villages with ancient stone packhorse bridges to lakes, tarns and craggy fells. Make the long and sometimes arduous climb to one of the region's many summits and you will be rewarded with unforgettable views like the one from the cairn at Pike O' Blisco (above). What better way to enjoy this unique scenery than from up on high, looking out onto the pyramid form of Bowfell and the surrounding mountains?

Whinfell Forest *left*

The Eden valley is an undiscovered corner of Cumbria. The river Eden rises at Mallerstang and flows into the Solway Firth north-west of Carlisle. The Settle to Carlisle railway follows the Eden valley, and yet it is unknown to all but a few discerning walkers. In the valley south-east of Penrith, in an often overlooked part of the Lake District, lies Whinfell Forest. This area of woodland, dense with Scots pine and Norwegian spruce, is a wildlife haven which abounds with a wide variety of flora and fauna. From the toadstools, wild mushrooms and heather that carpet the forest floor to the songs of cuckoos and bullfinches up high in the canopy of branches, Whinfell is full of delights and surprises at every turn. In 2004 a special red squirrel refuge was created in the forest, making Whinfell part of a vital network of conservation areas for these fascinating and much-loved animals. The forest is also home to extremely rare floral species including wild orchids.

Arnside *above & left*

Arnside sits on the estuary of the Kent river, where it meets Morecambe Bay near the Lancashire border. Its sands were famously crossed by Robert Bruce's men on their way to invade Lancashire in 1322. At one time Arnside was a bustling local port on the river with fishing fleets and mixed goods traffic of slate and pig iron. However, the building of the railway viaduct in 1857 caused the estuary to silt up, restricting shipping and transforming Arnside from a working coastal village to a holiday resort. From the promenade at Arnside there are stunning views across the estuary towards Grange and the peaks of the southern Lake District. The impressive viaduct was built by the Ulverston and Lancaster Railway Company; 1566ft (477m) long it is supported by 50 piers. Prior to the railway, the crossing of the bay relied upon an "over sands" coach service which ran from Ulverston to Lancaster. Today, you can still see vehicles using the sands, but now they are the carts belonging to the inshore fishing and shrimping workers.

Easdale Tarn

Situated in an isolated valley in the central Lake District fells close to Grasmere, Easdale contains one of the larger tarns in the Lake District. Climb the well-established rocky path from the village of Grasmere and walkers are rewarded with constantly changing views and wonderful scenery. Following the stream adjacent to the path brings them up past the dramatic sight of the raging Sourmilk Gill waterfall. William Wordsworth and his sister Dorothy were constant visitors to Easdale Tarn and referred to the area as "the black quarter", blaming it for all the bad weather that hit their home village of Grasmere.

The poet Thomas de Quincey described the tarn as a "Chapel within a Cathedral" and such is the striking beauty of the view across to the east and the snow-covered tops of the higher fells it is difficult not to agree. With impressive crags on three sides there is very much a sense of being in the heart of the mountains. The tarn itself lies in a basin carved during the ice age by glaciers and is 70ft (21m) deep. Beneath its mirror-like waters, reflecting the blue of a winter sky, there is a variety of freshwater fish such as perch, eels and brown trout.

Wasdale *above*

At 260ft (79m) Wast Water is the deepest lake in England. It lies in the remote Wasdale valley and at its deepest point is actually below sea level. Regarded by many as the most scenic of all the lakes, it presents a majestic panorama of the surrounding mountains of Red Pike, Kirk Fell, Great Gable and Scafell Pike. It is famous for the dramatic Wasdale Screes, a crumbling 1500ft (457m) high sheer wall of rock along the southern edge of the three-mile long lake. The nearby Wasdale Head Inn is a popular starting point for walks and climbs, and is often referred to as the birthplace of British climbing. Wast Water is the source of the river Irt which flows into the Irish Sea near Ravenglass.

The smallest church in England, St Olafs, is situated close to the hamlet of Wasdale Head and a stained-glass window in the church bears the inscription "I will lift up mine eyes unto the hills, from whence cometh my strength", a tribute to those climbers who have tackled the local peaks.

The Wasdale Show is held in the adjoining fields every October.

Fairfield *above & below*

The Fairfield Horseshoe is one of the most famous of the classic Lake District "rounds" and this challenging walk takes in all the peaks that surround the tiny hamlet of Rydal. The majority of the Lake District peaks are visible from the broad, grassy summit of Fairfield which is widely regarded as one of the best places to view Helvellyn. Although a popular walk, it is one that should only be undertaken in clear conditions as bad weather can make the route appear featureless and disorientating.

Eskdale Valley *right*

Eskdale is notable for being one of the few large valleys in the Lake District that does not have its own lake. The river Esk flows through the valley, water tumbling across its boulder-laden floor, all the way out to Ravenglass and into the Irish Sea. Looking east across the valley, one can see Hardknott Pass, the narrow and winding road that climbs to a height of 1289ft (393m), one of the steepest roads in Britain. Hardknott Roman Fort, near the top of the pass, provided commanding views for miles around.

Rydal Water *left*

At less than a mile long and the smallest of the region's lakes, Rydal Water is regarded by many as more of a tarn than a lake. Situated in the peaceful Rothay valley, it is connected to the neighbouring water of Grasmere by the river Rothay. Although surrounded by a number of popular fell walks, there is also a pleasant walk around the water's edge which takes in Dove Cottage, Rydal Cave and Wordsworth's Seat.

Derwent Water *below*

Known as "the Queen of the Lakes" Derwent Water is a three-mile long stretch of water with the popular town of Keswick at its northern end. With its wooded fells and tiny islands, and surrounded by some of the most magnificent scenery in the Lake District, it is a tranquil and peaceful lake with splendid shoreline walks. It is surrounded by some of the best-loved and well-known fells in the Lake District such as Skiddaw, Catbells and High Seat. Beautiful wooden launches ply the lake, starting from the Keswick boat landing and calling at six lakeshore jetties. There are splendid views of the fells and the many islands that grace Derwent Water including St Herbert's Island and Lord's Island, both of which are owned by the National Trust.

Grasmere *right*

Lying in the valley of Rothay, the lake at Grasmere is relatively small, about a mile long, with its own wooded island. A place particularly close to William Wordsworth's heart, he and his sister Dorothy are said to have regularly enjoyed picnics at this secluded spot. With its shallow, tree-lined grassy slopes, it is easy to see why he described it as "the loveliest spot that man hath ever found". There are rich descriptive names for many of the prominent features throughout the Lake District; looking up to Helm Crag one is presented with another example – the rocks at the summit here are known locally as "the Lion and the Lamb". From 1799 to 1808 the poet lived at Dove Cottage in the village of Grasmere; today the Wordsworth Museum is attached to the writer's former home.

Ullswater *above & below*

In the north-east of the region, Ullswater is the second largest lake in the Lake District at around nine miles (14.5km) long and with an average depth of 200ft (60m). Some say it is the most beautiful lake in Britain, and it is often referred to as "the English Lucerne". Less crowded than Windermere, Ullswater is extremely popular for sailing and there are anchorages and moorings dotted around its shoreline.

Brothers Water *right*

At the northern end of the Kirkstone Pass, High Hartsop Dodd is mirrored in the glittering lake at Brothers Water which lies just south of the much larger Ullswater. Formerly known as Broad Water, Brothers Water is reputed to have acquired its present name during the 19th century when two brothers drowned there. A quiet and tranquil lake compared to some of its larger counterparts, the shallow, reed-filled waters are renowned locally for their rich stocks of trout and pike. The village of Hartsop is located near the north-eastern corner of the lake. In the past this was a busy settlement with mining, quarrying and milling. On its western shore is Hartsop Hall, a 16th-century farmhouse which is now owned by the National Trust.

Thirlmere *above*

The growth of industry in and around Manchester increased the demand for water and, by the early 1890s, Manchester Corporation had identified Thirlmere as a potential source for additional water and erected a dam at the northern end of the lake. The valley was flooded and the two small existing lakes were amalgamated. With the increased volume, the water was then supplied to the city via the 100-mile long Thirlmere Aqueduct. Access to the lake is easy, especially from the quieter minor road on its western shore. When the valley was flooded the settlements of Armboth and Wythburn were both submerged and the only remaining building is the beautiful small whitewashed church in the shadow of Helvellyn.

The Langdale Pikes

The most prominent of the Langdale Pikes are Pike o' Stickle, Harrison Stickle and Pavey Ark which are situated at the southern end of Lakeland's central ridge. Alfred Wainwright's own description of the Pikes, that they are "once seen, never forgotten", is easy to agree with, not least because of the sense of scale they provide to the visitor. The Pikes' popularity lies in the wide variety of walks, from gentle climbs to technical scrambles. This view of the Pikes, looking across Stickle Tarn from near the dam, shows the rugged profile of Harrison Stickle and the steep rocky face of Pavey Ark. A popular scramble here is to ascend the 493ft (150m) face of Pavey Ark via the challenging and notorious route of "Jack's Rake", a narrow path which traverses the face of the mountain.

First published in 2009
by Myriad Books Limited,
35 Bishopsthorpe Road, London SE26 4PA

Photographs copyright © Simon Kirwan
Text copyright © Liam Kirwan

Liam Kirwan has asserted his right under the Copyright, Designs and Patents Act 1998 to be identified as the author of this work.

All rights reserved. No part of this publication may be reproduced, stored on a retrieval system, or transmitted in any form or by any means, electronic, mechanical, photocopying, recording or otherwise, without the prior permission of the copyright owners.

ISBN 1 84746 251 0
EAN 978 1 84746 251 0

Designed by Jerry Goldie Graphic Design

Printed in China

www.myriadbooks.com